The Queen's Pirate~
Francis Drake

Sarah Courtauld

Illustrated by Vincent Dutrait

History consultant: Michael Turner
Founder of the Drake Exploration Society

Francis Drake's voyages

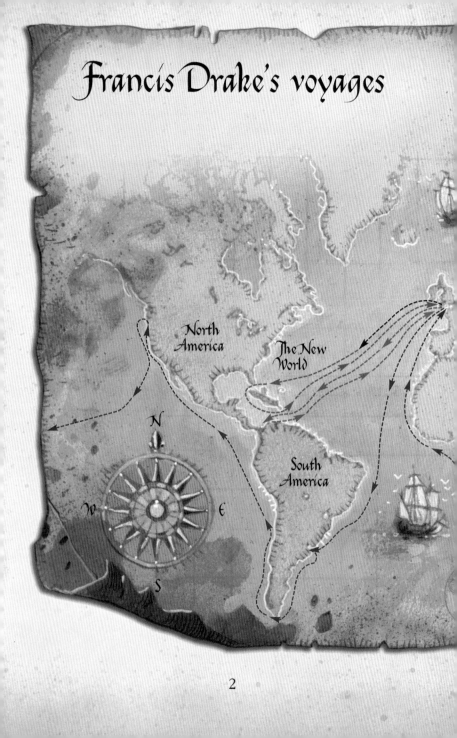

North America

The New World

South America

N

W

E

S

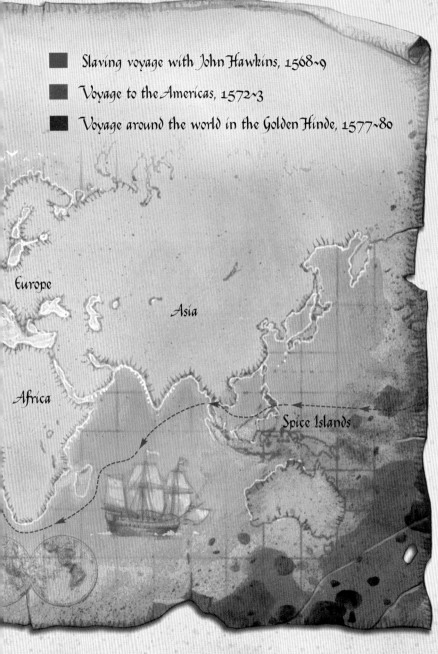

Slaving voyage with John Hawkins, 1568~9

Voyage to the Americas, 1572~3

Voyage around the world in the Golden Hinde, 1577~80

Europe

Asia

Africa

Spice Islands

Contents

Chapter 1

Francis Drake

"We live in dangerous but exciting times," said William Hawkins fiercely. "If you have courage, cunning and luck, you could make a great fortune at sea."

William's thin face was weathered by years on the oceans. His deep voice boomed out as he paced around his study, while his son John stood before him, hanging on his every word.

"I'll soon be setting sail on my next expedition," William said. "Now you are sixteen, you may come with me."

"Where are we sailing to?" asked John, wide-eyed.

"First we'll head to France," William replied, "to trade in the ports. But if we happen to come across a Spanish treasure ship on the way home…"

"Then we'll trade our goods for treasure?" asked John.

"No!" William laughed. "We'll capture the ship, and snatch the treasure for ourselves."

They didn't know that outside the study door, a little boy with a blaze of red hair was peering through the keyhole.

Eight-year-old Francis Drake pressed his forehead to the cold metal, and gazed through the narrow slit at his uncle and cousin, standing together in a pool of candlelight.

Francis wished they would let him go on the expedition with them. He wanted to feel the thrill of the high seas, to sail to faraway lands, to break open treasure chests and scoop up hundreds of gold coins in his hands. But he wasn't even allowed into his uncle's study – let alone across the oceans.

Francis watched intently as John turned to his father. "But looting from ships – surely that's no better than theft?" he blurted out.

"Theft!" William scoffed. "Do you know why Spain is the richest nation in the world? When the Spaniards conquered the New World, they found mines crammed full of gold and silver. Imagine that! A whole land, filled with more riches than you could ever dream of. Those toad-spotted Spanish rascals plundered it ruthlessly. But does it truly belong to them?"

"Perhaps not, but –"

"Besides," William went on, "Spain is England's enemy. Whatever we do to attack the Spaniards," William said passionately, "we do it for our Queen – and our country."

Francis didn't wait to hear any more. He ran swiftly and silently along the dark corridor, up the staircase to his room.

His mind was racing with all the things he had heard. He knew his uncle was a shipbuilder – but he had never guessed that he was a pirate.

Francis lay down on his small, cold bed. He had spent many nights wishing he was home again. His parents couldn't afford to bring him up themselves, so they had sent him to live with his uncle.

But now he realized how lucky he was. If he learned to be a pirate, he could win a great fortune. He would become a terror on the high seas, attacking enemy ships and winning all their gold. His uncle's words echoed in his mind as he fell asleep.

A year later, Francis' younger brother came to live in the Hawkins household too. Their cousin John had his own boats, and he let them go sailing as often as they liked. The higher the waves, the happier Francis was, with the wind in his face and salt spray flying past the bow.

Then at last, when he was eighteen, Francis was offered his first job. He was to be a purser, in charge of the finances on board his cousin's ship, the *Swallow*. Francis quickly became an expert seaman. After only a few years at sea, John Hawkins offered him a place on an expedition that would change his life.

Chapter 2

The New World

$\int$ n a dark corner of a noisy tavern, John explained his plan in a hushed voice.

"I'm sailing with a fleet of six ships. Queen Elizabeth herself is lending us one of her own, the *Jesus of Lubeck*," he said, "in return for a share of the profits, of course. I will captain the *Jesus*, and you'll sail on a smaller ship, the *Judith*."

"I've traded in ivory, gold, linen and spices," John went on. "But this is something new."

"So what will we sell?" Francis asked.

"People," John replied. "We'll kidnap villagers in Africa, and sell them as slaves in the New World, in return for precious treasure. Slavery is a profitable trade. When we return to England, we'll be rich."

Francis felt a thrill of excitement as he climbed onto the deck of the *Judith*. He'd been to Europe before, but now he was about to sail to an exotic, faraway continent – Africa. The *Judith* was the largest ship he'd ever set foot on. There were sailors everywhere – clambering up the rigging, coiling ropes and scrubbing the deck.

Francis climbed down under the
decks to explore the ship. Immediately the
smell hit him: the stench of animals mingled
with gunpowder and sweat. In one cabin, goats
were chained up in cages. In another, blacksmiths
were striking metal chains. He slung his bag into a
corner and scrambled up on deck as the boat
started to slip through the choppy water.

Within weeks, the fleet was moored off the coast of Guinea in West Africa. Francis and the other sailors rowed to the shore by moonlight, and then crept silently to the nearest village.

At a signal from John, they rushed in, grabbing screaming men and women from their beds.

Volleys of poisoned arrows rained down on the sailors. But they were no match for the sailors' swords. Within a few hours, the decks were crammed with hundreds of terrified people, who were thrown down into the blackness of the hold. They would never see their homes again.

After fifty-five days at sea, the journey was nearly over. Disease spread quickly in the *Judith's* filthy hold, and many of the slaves died. Up on deck, Francis stood at the tiller. Looking out through the mist, he saw a thin smudge on the horizon. He beamed and shouted to his crew, "Look – the shore of the New World!"

Once they had anchored, Francis and John sent a letter to the Spanish port commander, asking for permission to sell their slaves.

"You'll sell no slaves here," came the reply. "It is against the law to trade with the English."

John tore the letter to pieces. "I want 200 armed men on shore," he barked to his crew. "Set fire to buildings and take hostages."

Soon columns of thick black smoke snaked into the sky above the town.

"Buy our slaves," John wrote to the commander, "or we'll destroy the entire port."

The commander had no choice. The slaves were soon exchanged for gold and silver.

With its business done, the fleet sailed to a quiet bay. As the sun went down, Francis rowed over to the *Jesus*. John was pacing the deck nervously, eyeing a Spanish fleet moored nearby.

"They arrived here yesterday," he muttered to Francis. "I signed a truce with the Captain, and we've agreed there will be no attacks. But," he added, "I know the Spanish don't welcome us here. I don't trust them for a moment."

As he spoke, a shot tore through the main mast, and out of nowhere, a burning ship appeared. The Spaniards had set fire to one of their own ships and sent it drifting into the English fleet.

"Abandon ship!" Hawkins yelled, as flames raced up the rigging. "Those filthy Spanish dogs have betrayed us!"

John rowed to the nearest ship in his fleet, and gave orders for battle, while Francis raced back to the *Judith*.

"Now!" John bellowed, and the gunners fired their cannons. There was an almighty crash as the Spanish fleet returned the fire. Soon the sea looked like a seething cauldron. Sailors screamed as they tumbled headlong into the waves.

In the thick of the action, John peered through the smoke, and glimpsed the *Judith* speeding out of the bay.

"Francis –.you coward!" he gasped. In a moment, the *Judith* had vanished out of sight.

As the *Judith* raced away, Francis stood on deck, mad with rage. "At least those scheming Spaniards won't get their hands on my gold," he muttered to himself.

Francis vowed to get his revenge. One day he would return to the New World and steal a fortune in treasure from Spanish ships.

Chapter 3

Revenge

With his profits from the voyage, Francis was now wealthy enough to marry. He fell in love with a sweet-natured girl named Mary Newman and they were married near Plymouth, on July 4th, 1569. But if Mary was expecting him to settle down to married life, she was to be disappointed. Soon she was standing on the shore, sadly waving goodbye as Francis set out to sea once more.

Within weeks, Francis was back in the New World, working with English and French pirates to capture gold from Spanish ships. But for Francis it wasn't enough. He hatched a daring plan to hijack gold on its way from the mines to the coast.

Hundreds of African slaves, known as the Cimarrons, had fled their masters and were hiding out in the forests of the New World. They hated the Spaniards as much as Francis did, and readily agreed to help.

The Spaniards carried the gold along secret forest paths on packs of mules. The Cimarrons showed Francis where these hidden paths lay. One dark, cloudy night, Francis and his sailors crouched in the long grass, listening out for the jingling bells of the mules. For hours nothing stirred. Then, as dawn rose, they heard a faint sound in the distance. It came closer and closer...

The sailors leaped out of the shadows, scattering the Spanish soldiers.

"Take as much gold as you can carry," he shouted at his men, "and then run!"

A fierce skirmish followed, and some of his men fell to the path, badly wounded. But he didn't have time to save them. Clutching a sack of gold, he raced with the others through the dense jungle. When they reached the shore, the men stopped suddenly and looked out in dismay.

"Where's our ship?" a sailor cried. "It's vanished!" Instead, the sea was crawling with Spanish ships.

"Use this instead – and be quick," Francis ordered, tapping a tree trunk. At once the sailors chopped down several trees, made a raft out of wood and tore up sacks to make a sail. Grabbing the gold, they set off across the bay to a nearby island.

The next day, they all waved and shouted as Drake's ship sailed into view. The ship's crew had been hiding from the Spaniards. But they had come back to rescue Francis and his men.

On his return to England, stories quickly spread about England's most successful pirate. While he went on more expeditions, King Philip of Spain wrote furious letters to Queen Elizabeth.

"You must arrest this murderous thief. I demand the return of all my gold."

"I will certainly punish Drake," she agreed. Then she summoned Francis to see her in London.

Francis' footsteps echoed through the dark, empty corridors of the palace.

"The Queen might arrest me at any moment," he thought, shuddering. "I could win ten thousand battles at sea, but she would still hold my life in her hands." When he reached the Queen's room, he bowed low before her.

"Drake," she said, "I have told King Philip
that I am going to punish you. But, whatever I say
in public, you will always have my private
support. I have brought you here in secret
because I have a plan that's going to make both
our fortunes. And nobody – not even my closest
advisors – can know of it."

"I'll do anything you wish, Your Majesty,"
Francis replied, overwhelmed with relief.

"Take a fleet of ships to South America," ordered
the Queen. "From there, you will sail on to discover
new lands. Bring me back great riches. If you
succeed, you will be known throughout the world as
a daring explorer."

Chapter 4

Around the world

On December 13th, 1577, Drake set sail on the Queen's mission in charge of a fleet of six ships. He sailed on the largest, the *Pelican*, and the journey started well. Francis had a fine crew, and he was delighted that his younger brother was on board with him. On Christmas day, they anchored in Morocco. Then the fleet set out on its long journey across the rolling Atlantic.

Sometimes the sailors were lucky and caught a dolphin or a flying fish to eat. Other times, they had to eat stinking, maggot-ridden meat and old biscuits. Some sailors ate their biscuits in the dark, so they couldn't see the worms inside them.

On windless days,
when the sea was as
smooth as glass, the
crew passed the time
on deck, playing
draughts or singing
sea shanties.

As time passed, Francis began to have nagging doubts about a member of his crew, Thomas Doughty. He was a wealthy officer, in charge of one of the smaller ships, the *Mary*.

"I'm sure he's after my position," Francis thought, as he watched Doughty approach his cabin. He gritted his teeth as he welcomed him inside.

"I- I'm sorry to tell you this," Doughty began warily, "but I've caught your brother stealing goods from the ship's hold."

"He wouldn't do such a thing," Francis snapped. "It's just as I guessed," he thought to himself. "He's trying to undermine me, and he's using my brother to do it."

Francis strode up to Thomas and grabbed his arm. "My brother will take your position as Captain of the *Mary*," he hissed. "Now get out of my sight."

Long after Doughty had gone, Francis was still sitting silently in his cabin. "What if Doughty tries to turn the crew against me?" he thought. "Well, I won't give him the chance."

As the fleet neared South America, the sky darkened. Rain lashed the deck of the *Pelican* and the ship crashed on through the dark seas, creaking and thrashing in the water like a wounded animal.

"Doughty is a witch," Francis shouted to his chaplain, over the roaring wind. "The storm clouds are flying out of his cap. He'll drown us all."

"But Captain –"

"Have him brought to the *Pelican* and strapped to the mast."

When the storms had passed, Francis anchored in Argentina and announced that he was putting Doughty on trial for mutiny. He brought the whole crew ashore for the trial. Doughty was found guilty.

Two days later, he knelt quietly before the executioner's block and was beheaded.

"This is the end of traitors!"
Drake thundered, holding up
Doughty's severed head. "If any of
you wants to go home, you can take
the smallest ship. But if I
catch you, I'll sink you."
No one would dare
disobey Drake now.

Weeks later, in the dead of the night, Francis sat bolt upright in bed, his eyes wild with terror. Doughty was gone – but Francis panicked as he remembered a close friend of Doughty's – Sir Christopher Hatton.

"When Hatton hears about this, he'll be furious. And he's one of the most powerful men in England." Francis had to think quickly. "Perhaps I could flatter him into silence," he said softly to himself.

The next day, Drake had the carpenters carve a new figurehead – the golden head of a female deer. "The *Pelican* will be renamed the *Golden Hinde*, after Sir Christopher Hatton's coat of arms," he announced proudly to the crew.

The fleet sailed on round the coast of South America. For weeks, it cruised through calm, blue seas. But, as they reached Chile, they were battered by fierce winds, and two of Drake's ships were lost in the storm. Francis stared out to sea. He kept hoping to see their sails on the horizon. But the ships had vanished.

As they continued their journey north, Drake's crew looted each village they passed. The sailors sent a tremor of terror up the coast of Peru. The villagers thought that Drake must be a sorcerer, or even the devil himself.

Soon Drake realized that his fleet was too large for the swift work of raiding and looting. He brought all his crew and cargo onto the *Golden Hinde* and abandoned his other ships. Like a ghostly fleet, the empty ships drifted out to sea.

As they entered the port of Callao, Drake heard that a Spanish treasure ship, the *Cacafuego*, lay just two weeks' sail ahead.

"A gold chain to the first person to spot it," he announced. Everyone scanned the horizon as the ship rolled through deep blue seas.

One afternoon, from high up in the cross trees, the lookout yelled – "I see a sail!"

The *Golden Hinde* crept up on the *Cacafuego*.

"Take down your sails!" Francis yelled across to the *Cacafuego*.

The *Cacafuego*'s captain, San Juan de Anton, stood proudly on deck. "What Englishman demands that I take down my sails?" he roared back. "Take them down yourself!"

"Fire!" Francis ordered, and his sailors blasted the cannons. The first shot smashed the *Cacafuego's* main mast in two. Then the *Golden Hinde's* archers scrambled up the masts and sent arrows flying through the air.

Captain Anton looked on in shock as Drake's sailors climbed up the sides of his ship, and swarmed onto the decks. Drake was the first English sailor in these waters. The crew of the *Cacafuego* hadn't expected to be attacked, so they had no weapons to defend the ship.

The fight was soon won. Francis' men broke
open the *Cacafuego's* treasure chests. There were
thirteen caskets of silver, jewels and precious
stones – Francis' fortune was made.

Anton was dragged back to the *Golden Hinde* as a prisoner. He did not expect any mercy from his captors. But as he stepped, trembling, onto the deck, Francis smiled broadly at him. "Welcome to the *Golden Hinde*. Come and dine at my table."

A few days later, Francis waved him goodbye. He left him on the coast with a silver bowl and a letter of safe passage. Anton never forgot Drake's kindness.

The *Golden Hinde* continued its journey to find new lands. But, as the ship sailed north, the weather grew colder and colder, and the ship became shrouded in thick white fog.

One morning, Francis awoke to see that puddles of water all over the deck had frozen into shimmering ice.

He took a deep breath of freezing air that cut his lungs. "It's too cold to go any further north," he barked at his pilot. "The Pacific lies to the west, and the *Golden Hinde* will be the first English ship to cross it."

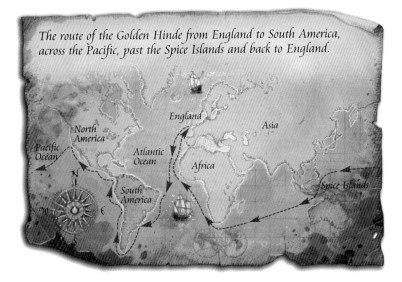

The route of the Golden Hinde from England to South America, across the Pacific, past the Spice Islands and back to England.

But the *Golden Hinde* would have to be taken ashore and cleaned before it was ready for the long journey home. So the pilot pulled the tiller hard to the left. The sails flapped and the ship turned a graceful arc in the water. Soon a row of white cliffs loomed ahead. Inch by inch, the crew dragged the ship onto the beach, and then scrubbed the thick, stinking mud off the hull.

Before they left, Drake hammered a stake into the ground. "I claim this land for Queen Elizabeth," he declared. "I call it New England."

The next morning, the ship sailed out of the bay, rolling slowly over gentle waves. The bright blue Pacific lay ahead. They were finally going home.

After crossing the
Pacific, the *Golden Hinde*
slowly wound its way through
the Spice Islands, where Francis
bought chests of cloves, cinnamon
and ginger. Then it carried on its
journey west, passing strange,
unknown islands. One was teeming
with giant crabs that scuttled up and
down the trees. As they sailed past,
there was a rush of beating
wings, as a flock of
bats spiralled over
the ship.

On September 26th, 1580, after three years at sea, the crew raised a huge cheer as they spotted the port of Plymouth.

The following spring, jostling crowds lined the streets as the Queen herself arrived to visit Drake on board his ship. She stepped onto the deck and watched as Drake was knighted. Now he was Sir Francis Drake and a national hero. He had sailed all around the world, and brought back vast hordes of gold and silver for the Queen.

Chapter 5

The Armada

"He's a villainous, dog-hearted rascal," whispered Burghley, the Queen's treasurer.

"He's nothing more than a common thief," Lord Sussex replied. "The Spaniards call him *El Draco* – the Dragon. Every time he sets fire to another Spanish ship, he enrages King Philip more and more. And now England is moving steadily closer to war."

The courtiers fell silent as they saw Drake approach, but he barely glanced at them. He knew that some of them disliked him, but he didn't let it bother him.

After all, he had charmed the Queen. He lived in an enormous house called Buckland Abbey. And after his first wife died, he had married Elizabeth Sydenham, who was young, wealthy and beautiful.

"I've got all the luck in the world," he thought, sweeping past them into the Great Hall.

51

"If only the Queen would listen to reason, not to that hot-headed fool," said Lord Sussex, once Drake was gone.

"It's far too late for that," replied Burghley. "Spain is now our deadly enemy."

A year later, England was preparing for war.

"The Spanish fleet is planning to invade us," Elizabeth declared, "and I will lead my people to a famous victory."

Drake was made Vice-Admiral of the English fleet, under Lord Howard. Drake's cousin, John Hawkins, was put in charge of designing new, faster ships, to beat the Spanish galleons.

Once the ships were ready, the only thing left to do was to wait for the Spanish fleet – the Armada – to appear over the horizon.

On July 19th, 1588, the Armada was spotted. More than a hundred galleons stretched out in a line, like a floating city of golden castles.

The Spanish ships advanced straight into the English fleet, close enough for their soldiers to try to board the English ships. But the English fought them off, blasting their cannons at them as they sailed past. Fierce battles raged for days.

The naval commanders met one evening to discuss their battle plans.

"I have an idea," said Francis with a grin, "that could send the Armada flying into a panic, like a fox among chickens. And it just might work."

In the dead of night, he ordered his men to set fire to eight empty English ships. Then they sent them drifting into the darkness, in the direction of the Armada.

The Spaniards awoke to see huge towers of fire racing towards them across the black water. Terrified, the Spanish ships fled until they were scattered out across the sea.

Drake followed hard on their heels. He stared grimly ahead, as the driving rain spat in his face. The ship lurched through the darkness over waves as steep as cliffs. At last he was close enough to fire his cannons, and the ships were drawn together in a bloody clash.

Soon both fleets were ablaze, and the air
thundered with cannonfire. The battle lasted for
two exhausting weeks. Finally the Spanish fleet was
defeated, scattered by savage storms across the
North Sea. Many Spanish sailors drowned as
their ships were wrecked along the
Scottish and Irish coasts.

Francis returned to see the Queen.

"I want you to do as much damage to the retreating fleet as you can," she ordered, "so they can never threaten our shores again."

Francis set off to carry out her orders, but he soon changed his plans. If he helped a nobleman called Dom Antonio to win the Portuguese throne, he could win plunder for himself. Ignoring the Queen's orders, he sailed to Portugal.

The expedition was a disaster. The plan failed, many of his crew died of disease, and Francis returned to England, utterly miserable. He had destroyed very few ships from the Spanish fleet... and Queen Elizabeth was livid.

"You seem to care more about lining your pockets than serving your country," she snapped, eyeing him coldly.

Drake managed to escape punishment, but Elizabeth never trusted him again.

Chapter 6

The last voyage

Francis expected to live the rest of his life in England, but his cousin John had other ideas.

"I'm finding a crew for one final, glorious voyage," John told him. "I'm sailing to Puerto Rico, to loot a treasure ship."

John Hawkins was an old man now. His hair was white and he walked with a limp. But his eyes were still gleaming.

"I want you to come with me," he said, and Francis agreed at once. They gathered a fleet of twenty-seven ships and set sail on August 28th, 1595. But Francis and John fought bitterly.

Then, just before they reached Puerto Rico, John became sick and died shortly afterwards.

Days later, Francis was raising a toast at dinner, when his stool was shot from under him. It was a surprise attack from guns on shore.

Francis sped into the bay and hurled firebombs at the Spanish ships. But, as the targets caught fire, they lit up the whole port. Now the Spanish gunners on shore could see Drake's ships perfectly.

"Retreat!" Francis roared to his sailors.

They escaped – by a hair's breadth.

"I'm not giving up now," Francis said grimly to his crew. "Sail on to Panama – we'll find gold there."

As his ship glided slowly over the water, murky air drifted over the boat, creeping in through the hatches and lingering in the hold. Fever spread through the crew and many sailors died.

Soon Francis was taken ill, too. He lay, sweating and shivering in his cabin, as the fever wracked his body. In the middle of the night he cried out.

"I want to die like a soldier," he said. But as he was being dressed for battle, he swayed, crumpled back into his bed, and died.

Cannons shot out as Francis Drake's coffin was lowered into the cold, grey ocean.

His luck had finally run out.

My life at sea

1540	I am born in Tavistock, in Devon.
1558-66	I go on my first voyages with my cousin John Hawkins.
1568	I go on a slaving voyage with John Hawkins to Guinea and the New World.
1568	The Spaniards attack at San Juan de Ulua, Mexico.
1569	I marry Mary Newman.
1577-80	I sail around the world.
1581	I return to England and am knighted by Queen Elizabeth.
1583	My wife, Mary Drake, dies, childless.
1585	I marry the beautiful Elizabeth Sydenham.
1588	England defeats the Armada, with my help.
1589	My expedition to Lisbon is a terrible failure.
1595-6	I sail on my last voyage to the Caribbean. I must face my death at sea.

Index

Internet links

For links to websites where you can find out more
about Francis Drake go to the Usborne Quicklinks Website at
www.usborne-quicklinks.com and type the keywords
YR Francis Drake.
The recommended websites are regularly reviewed and updated
but, please note, Usborne Publishing is not responsible for
the content of websites other than its own.

Designed by Andrea Slane
Edited by Jane Chisholm

First published in 2007 by Usborne Publishing Ltd,
Usborne House, 83-85 Saffron Hill, London EC1N 8RT, England. www.usborne.com